WHERE WAS GOD?

UNDERSTANDING THE HOLOCAUST IN THE
LIGHT OF GOD'S SUFFERING

STEPHEN D. MORRISON

BELOVED PUBLISHING · COLUMBUS, OHIO

Printed in the United States of America

Published by Beloved Publishing: Columbus, Ohio

ISBN: 978-1-63174-082-4

CONTENTS

1

A NEW TOPIC

To begin, let me introduce the four individuals who will take part in this discussion: Jurgen, Jean, Friedrich, and Clive are all professors at a local university. It doesn't matter which one particularly, but it may be helpful to know the field of study each is in. Jurgen is the theologian of the bunch, and seeing that this book is about theology you'll probably be hearing the most from him. Jean is a mathematician, Friedrich is an anthropologist, and Clive is a professor of English literature. These professors all meet semi-regularly at the campus coffee shop to discuss some of their common academic interests.

Not much more really needs to be said in terms of an introduction. You'll soon begin to learn about them more personally, and the topic of discussion will also become apparent.

In a coffee shop.

Clive: You know, Jean, I think you might be right about Dostoyevsky. I had never seen it before, but it does seem like the whole work centers around that conversation between Ivan and Alyosha (*Brothers Karamazov*). What is said there seems to echo throughout the rest of the book. The clash of skepticism and belief is apparent, but that specific conversation does seem to be central to what Dostoyevsky is all about.

Jean: Thank you, Clive. And yes, I'm convinced it is. No other scene seems to give such a summary.

Friedrich: But what of that famous statement Ivan makes? I know you're both men of faith, but in my observation, it seems like Ivan plays a trump card against Alyosha. His argument for skepticism is one of the best.

Jurgen: Sorry to cut in, but what is this famous statement you're talking about Friedrich? It's been quite some times since I read the book.

Friedrich: Yes, of course. Let me see if I can find it in my notes. Ah, here it is. Part II, book V, chapter III:

> It's not that I don't accept God, you must understand, it's the world created by Him I don't and cannot accept. Let me make it plain. I believe like a child that suffering will be healed and made up for, that all the humiliating absurdity of human contradictions will vanish like a pitiful mirage, like the despicable fabrication of the impotent and infinitely small Euclidian mind of man, that in the world's finale, at the moment of eternal harmony, something so precious will come to pass that it will suffice for all hearts, for the comforting of all resentments, for the atonement of all the crimes of humanity, of all the blood they've shed; that it will make it not only possible to forgive but to justify all that has happened with men—but though all that may come to pass, I don't accept it. I won't accept it.

Another important statement which summarizes Ivan's point, if you don't mind me reading it as well, comes from the next chapter (chapter VI):

> And so I hasten to give back my entrance ticket, if I am an honest man I am bound to give it back as soon as possible. And that I am doing. It's not God that I don't accept, Alyosha, only I must respectfully return Him the ticket.

Jean: Those Russian writers sure knew how to say things with elegance. And this is exactly my point, Clive, as we discussed before coming here today. I think this conversation marks the central position Dostoyevsky is trying to make. Here Ivan presents the best argument an Atheist could ever make against the existence of God. If one is honest, it's really the only position an atheist could take.

Friedrich: I'm afraid you might be right on that, although I wouldn't go as far as to say it's the only reason for becoming an Atheist. I personally reject God because I believe that there is no logical way for such a being to coexist with humanity. Sure, God may exist, as Ivan said, I do accept this fact, but so what? Even if God exists, He or She or It would not be a God I'd like to know! I mean this world is dark and evil, humanity has made it so. What sort of God would put us in a place like this? And sure, you might say that we are to blame and God is just giving up what we deserve by being here, but do little children deserve to pay for the sins of their fathers? Do the victims of child molestation really "deserve" to suffer? What sort of God would let this world exist? If I were God, I would not make a world with such tragedy. I believe that Ivan is right in this regard: God is acceptable, but the world is not. I "accept" God if I must, but I cannot accept the world God has made.

Jurgen: I think we may have found our next topic. Thanks to you Clive and Jean for bringing it up. I think Friedrich's comments are fair, being the only atheist in the group, he offers a helpful perspective for us all, wouldn't you agree?

Jean: Certainly. But I think if we're going to go down this road we should be clear about what we're getting into. If I understand you correctly Jurgen, you'd like to have the Theodicy conversation?

Jurgen: Yes, that's right. I know it was bound to come up eventually. I doubt there's a person alive who hasn't asked the theodicy question. But perhaps we should be less general? Let's avoid abstract discussions, those rarely lead to anything. Let's make this practical, that way...

Clive: No, let's make it historical!

Friedrich: What do you mean Clive?

Clive: I'm sorry for bursting in like that Jurgen, but I think I have

just come up with a great idea! I agree we should avoid being too
abstract, especially when such an important issue is being discussed,
but being practical might eventually become too personal. Let's be
historical then, that way we can look objectively at a historical event
and discuss it without having any emotional ties to the event.

Jurgen: Good point. What did you have in mind?

Clive: I think the Holocaust is a perfect topic for us. It's far
enough away from each of us in years, yet it's close enough to matter.
That way we remain objectively unemotional, yet subjectively serious.
We know how real and tragic the Holocaust was, but none of us
personally experienced it. We then have no ties to the outcome of the
discussion, yet we will take it seriously enough to do all the necessary
research.

Friedrich: I think that's a great idea, Clive. So that settles it. Our
new topic of discussion will be God and the Holocaust.

Jean: How about, "Where was God in the Holocaust?" Because I
believe in the face of human suffering, this is really the only question
that matters. Victims rarely ask philosophical questions; they ask
personal ones. For example: "Why has God, who loves me, abandoned
me in my suffering? Where was God?" This, I believe, is the most
elementary cry of humanity in the midst of suffering. So I think it's
how we should frame our discussion.

Jurgen: Yes, I like it. I see a great discussion brewing over this one!
Who'd want to start? I think we should go about this in our usual
format. First, we each present our opening positions about the present
dilemma, then some brief cross discussion, and finally we return once
again, having researched and thought it all out, to discuss further our
conclusions.

Friedrich: Yes, but Jurgen, you seem to be at an advantage here.
Remember a few weeks ago when we discussed Shakespeare? You
suggested that Clive, as a professor of English Literature, should act
more as a moderator of sorts. Not that you can't say anything, but give
us a chance to present our opinions before you present yours at least.
How about that? What if the three of us present our positions, and
then you critique them? In the light of your critique, we research a
little and come back later to hash it out again. Then in the final

sessions, you unveil your position. That'll perhaps give us a fighting chance, seeing that God is a profession of yours.

Jurgen: Well, I'm not so sure about calling it a profession. I don't think that's fair to say. Who can be a professional at "God"? Hah, but I see you're point. Although I would rather say, we're all on equal footing here—because who among us can say they know God well enough to answer such a question? However, it is my job to have read all there is to learn about subjects like this. So I guess that does give me somewhat of an advantage, I agree. But how about everyone else, does this sound fair?

Clive: Sure, I think it'll help keep us sharp.

Jean: Agreed.

Friedrich: Great then. Jean, how about you get us started?

Jean: Okay, sure thing. I'd say my position's reasonably simple. Since God is God and God is sovereign, we must say that the Holocaust was a part of His Divine will. Somehow, however mysterious it may seem, God willed for the Holocaust event to happen. I can't say to know why God let it happen, but I have to say that He did. He is God after all, and in His sovereignty, God is free to do as He pleases. As the Apostle Paul wrote, "'Jacob I loved, but Esau I hated.' What shall we say then? Is there injustice on God's part? By no means! For God says to Moses, 'I will have mercy on whom I have mercy, and I will have compassion on whom I have compassion.'" (That's Romans 9:13-15 for the record.) Here Paul is giving a clear answer to the question of theodicy: God's will is sovereign; God is in control; "all things are predetermined by the good pleasure of God's will." (Calvin)

So what can I say about the Holocaust event? What can anyone say? God is God, and we are evil men. However unjust or un-"fair" it may sound to some, the fact remains that God can do whatever God wants even if that means the Holocaust. God is free to predetermine such an event to take place and we cannot question His will.

I can't shake this position because any alternatives are just unthinkable. God is sovereign, and therefore He willed the Holocaust event. If He did not will the Holocaust event, then God is not sovereign. Therefore, I believe this is the only logical conclusion we can make. Although we cannot say why the Holocaust happened, we must say that it happened as a part of God's sovereign will for the human race. That's my position.

Friedrich: Let me see if I understand you, Jean. Are you saying that God caused the Holocaust?

Jean: Well, yes and no. I suppose it's fair to say that the Nazi's caused the Holocaust, but more importantly, God willed it. Human beings might have performed the act, but God is the sovereign Lord of all history. I guess then I would say that God indirectly caused the Holocaust and that although He did not kill all those people, He willed for them to die. In fact, since it was in His will, it was also His pleasure. He predetermined the Holocaust event as a part of His sovereign plan for humanity. In the end, we will all see how it was for our good, and that God had a plan all along. So we have to trust Him and trust in His plan for the human race.

Clive: But wouldn't that logically imply that Hitler was a good man, simply doing God's will?

Jean: Well, no. It doesn't mean that the evil done by Hitler is justified. Like Pharaoh in the Exodus of Egypt, Hitler's heart was hardened by God in order to carry out His Divine will. Hitler was a pawn; I suppose we could say, through whom God displayed His power. Paul himself goes on in that passage to say this very thing. Let me read it for you: "For the scripture says to Pharaoh, 'for this very purpose I have raised you up, that I might show my power in you, and that my name might be proclaimed in all the earth.' So then God has mercy on whomever he wills, and he hardens whomever he wills" (V. 17-18). It was God's will to harden the heart of Pharaoh, and therefore it was also fair and just of God to harden the heart of Hitler in our day. I believe the parallel between these two figures is clear.

Clive: But doesn't that make God the cause of inequity? How can it be just for God to send Hitler to hell for something He willed in the first place? That flips the whole Christian idea of salvation on its head, doesn't it?

Jean: Ah! You don't seem familiar with this passage Clive, or you would know that Paul answers that very question next. "You will say to me then, 'why does he still find fault? For who can resist his will?' But who are you, O man, to answer back to God? Will what is molded say to its molder, 'why have you made me like this?' Has the potter no right over the clay, to make out of the same lump one vessel for honorable use and another for dishonorable use? What if God, desiring to show his wrath and to make known his power, has endured with much patience vessels of wrath prepared for destruction, in order to make known the riches of his glory for vessels of mercy, which he has prepared beforehand for glory" (V. 19-23). You see friend, God is God, and who are you, a mere man, to question His will? Who are you to question the justice of God?

Clive: But I'm afraid you're taking that out of context...

Friedrich: Okay, okay. Sorry to break in, but you'll have your chance to offer a rebuttal later, Clive. For now, let's move on. I'll present my position next.

I have to agree with what Richard Rubenstein has said about this dilemma. He saw that there is only one logically consistent response to the Holocaust: Atheism. In the light of such a monstrosity, one can only reject God outright. There can be no belief in God post-Auschwitz. In order for such an event to take place in history it must mean that there has never been a God, to begin with. God is dead, friends, and we have killed him. God must be dead in this world if we are to progress as a society. What sort of God allows the Holocaust to happen? It's clearly unethical to imagine any sort of God who would let the holocaust happen, or worst yet, as in Jean's position, a God who took pleasure in the Holocaust! Such a God is a monster, and I would rather reject this God completely than live a life of service to him. If there is a hell, I will happily go there with the solace that I told the truth. God is unjust if God exists. Therefore, God must not exist, and we must be Gods ourselves. I'll say it again: God is dead.

As Ivan said too, in Dostoyevsky's novel, God is possible, abstractly, but as soon as you take into consideration the present evil world we live in, God is impossible. There is not God post-Holocaust. This is my position. Jean, although I respect you, your position makes me sick. If I'm honest, it makes my position seems far more appealing to me. Your God is a monster, my friend, and for that reason, I feel ethically responsible to reject God entirely.

And I know, before you say it, that "God is God" and we can't claim to know the mysteries of His sovereign will. But let me ask you this: If God is unethical, and I believe your God is, how could we know it? Wouldn't it be that we were given ethics by your God (if He exists)?

Jean: But no, that's not true at all. God is different than us. Where did you get your idea of ethics? If ethics matter so much to you, why not ask where your ethics come from? God defines what is ethical. That doesn't mean that we can claim ourselves as more ethical than Him just because we disagree or misunderstand His ways. What you have done here is you've claimed your own ethics as objective truth. But what if your ethics are not ethical at all? Only God is truly good, and therefore who's to say what is ethical or unethical besides Him? Your position hardly makes God unethical, for who are you, a mere man, to talk back to the absolute God? We are but grass in the wind, dust to dust we go but God remains forever.

Friedrich: Okay, okay. I see your point. Hypothetically you might be right. But I still think if you are right, I would rather be in hell than be in heaven with a God who kills people just for the fun of it. An eternity in hell would be paradise compared to a single moment with your monster God. But like I said, we can save these rebuttals for later. Let's move on. Clive, I want to hear what you have to say.

Clive: Thank you, Friedrich. I guess I'll begin with an attempt to find a way between both of your positions. I would agree with Friedrich that ethically speaking God is not a monster and we cannot create a system which necessitates this sort of thinking. But I would also echo Jean in saying that we can only know what is just and unjust if there is, in fact, an origin for this moral compass. Where do we get the notion of justice and injustice? It must be from God. And I know you say, Friedrich, that if we are more just than God we are greater than God Himself. However, I would not say that God is unjust. My position is that God did not will the Holocaust or cause it to happen. Therefore, your defense that God is unjust cannot stand here. God is just, and the fact that you argue with justice in mind proves the fact that God exists. For where else could you deduce the nature of justice or injustice if there is no God? All would be relative and your argument would be equally invalid.

So in my position, I will attempt to bridge the gap. I at once will agree and disagree with both of you. I agree with Jean that God does exist, for I feel this is the only logical conclusion one can make. (Although that's a discussion for another time.) However, I disagree, Jean, with your monster God. Such a God completely negates the existence of free will. I would say instead that God gives humanity suffering as a consequence for their sins. Suffering then acts as a megaphone to wake up the sleeping world to the righteousness of God. Which does not mean that God caused suffering or the Holocaust. Instead, God is a chess player smart enough to make use of suffering and pain in order to help humanity on our progressive journey.

Therefore, I affirm Friedrich's critique of Jean's monster God, while negating Friedrich's atheism. In summary, then, I will say that God did not cause the Holocaust, and therefore any Atheism which is founded upon the existence of evil is irrational and self-contradictory in that it affirms the existence of an absolute morality. The only logical response then is to say that God exists, and the Holocaust was not God's fault. Evil itself is a mystery that cannot logically be the basis of any argument, and therefore I feel that both of your positions are flawed in that they are based on the unknowable relationship between evil and God.

Jurgen: Interesting, Clive, I've always enjoyed your rigorous conclusions, but what do you say to our original dilemma? In your line of thinking, can you give an answer to "where was God in the Holocaust?" In my opinion, you seem to be defending God, and I know you would consider yourself an apologist so this doesn't surprise me, but I don't see your position as true theodicy. You may defend God in this way, but that is not our dilemma. What is your answer to the problem of the Holocaust event and the omnipotence of a sovereign God? Where was God, if God really is all loving and powerful, in the midst of the Holocaust?

Clive: Of course, and thank you for the compliment. I believe that your question is unanswerable. I know that God did not cause the Holocaust, for it is an event contrary to His nature. I know that evil is an inconsistent and irrational thing and therefore cannot be factored into the arguments of God and truth. I also know that God must exist if morals are true and real. But as to your question, I must "plead the fifth." I do not know, nor do I believe anyone else can know, where God was in the Holocaust event. It is a mystery of which we cannot have a firm understanding. Here I agree with Jean: God is God, and we are human. This dilemma is a mystery which only God can know, and it is therefore not something we can actually speak about. So I would say our original position is flawed, in that the theodicy question is unanswerable.

Jurgen: Alright, fair enough. You never were one for simple answers, Clive. So then, friends, allow me to summarize your positions before we continue. Jean, you've taken—oh let's call it the Determinist position: that God predetermined the Holocaust event in His sovereign will. Friedrich, you've claimed atheism as the only logical response to the Holocaust dilemma. And Clive, in an attempt to bridge the gap between these two positions, you've stated that God did not cause the Holocaust and therefore atheism has no rational reason to reject the existence of God. However, you've held that the original dilemma an unanswerable question due to the otherness of God. What shall we call your position? A Cliveian system?

Clive: An appeal to unknowing, I'd prefer, but if you feel inclined to call it that you may. Although I am certainly not the first one to produce such an answer!

Jurgen: Alright then. Well, we're almost out of time. I've decided to keep my critiques of your positions to myself until next week. For now, I want to hear your rebuttals. Let's keep them simple. I've got a class in thirty minutes across campus. Let's have your brief position against the other two positions. Since you've gone last Clive, you can start.

Clive: Alright. I've stated my rebuttals some already, but I'll make a few more points here. To Jean: I think your understanding of Romans 9 is flawed. You have failed to take into consideration the overall context of the verse, which is Paul discussing the salvation of Israel. Paul in that passage is not presenting a case for determinism as you've imposed into it, rather he is discussing the fact that God is free to save the Gentiles in spite of the Jews, and that eventually, as Romans 11 concludes, God will save His people Israel. Instead of being a passage of such black and white determinism, this is a complex passage in the overall conversation of Jewish salvation and Gentile inclusion. This point is clear right where you stopped in the passage. In verse 24 Paul continues to say that "not only from the Jews only but also from the Gentiles?" meaning God prepared from before time to include the Gentiles into the salvation of the Jewish people. The passage Paul quotes from Hosea makes this context even clearer. Paul isn't talking about how God is going to determine some over others. Instead, He is arguing why it is just for God to include all people, even the Gentiles, into the salvation of Jesus Christ.

And Friedrich, I believe that your position is based too much upon evil-centered logic. You have deduced that God does not exist because evil does exist, but this is a flawed way of thinking. Evil cannot be the center of your thought, because evil in and of itself is irrational. Evil cannot determine why God is or isn't. It can only be understood as an enigma. Anything beyond that is to "play God," but I'm afraid you've already admitted to that assertion yourself.

Jurgen: Okay, thanks, Clive. You're next Friedrich.

Friedrich: Thanks. I suppose most of what I wanted to say has been said already. However, I do believe I've been misinterpreted in your arguments. Atheism is not anti-moralism. I don't believe that truth is relative, and if I did this whole argument would be self-contradictory! So, Clive, I am afraid your argument against atheism is flawed. It's not true that ethics point to a God of an ethical nature. You're failing to consider the social element of ethics. Humanity is not a group of independent individuals. We are a series of tribes. Each tribe thinks alike, has similar morals, and even similar Gods. To say that your particular ethics point to your specific God is to err. Not every ethical system of thought in every tribe points to your same God. What about the Buddhists in India? Or what about the isolated tribes without any modern contact who practice cannibalism? Who is to say that their socially constructed ethical code does not equally point to an ethical God as yours does? You see Clive, your argument works within our current tribe, but as soon as you take into consideration the overall history of humanity it is nearly impossible to deduce the existence of God from ethical codes. Tribes have always disagreed with other tribes. Therefore your argument of universal ethics is inconsistent and flawed.

And Jean, I hold to my statements that your God is a monster-God who, if exists, I would happily suffer in hell if that means being far, far away from your God. I don't care if I'm wrong as an atheist, you cannot be right. And if you are, I will happily accept hell and pity those in heaven who suffer a life with such a monster God.

Jurgen: Thanks, Friedrich. Back to you Jean, your final rebuttal?

Jean: Thanks, Jurgen. I concede that perhaps the picture of God I have projected is not a fair one, but I also hold to my position. God is God, and we are not. Therefore, we cannot question His mysterious ways. It may be "unethical" to believe in such a God, but I see no other option. Clive, you have failed to take the scripture at hand seriously. Romans 9 cannot be wished away with such simple reasoning. It may be true what you are saying, but the verses I've stated still stand in opposition to your overall case. God is perfectly free to cause and take delight in the Holocaust event and that is a just thing for Him to do. If He has done it, then it is just indeed. Our finite minds cannot know God's infinite magnitude. Therefore, to speak of God as if He were one of us is to error gravely! This is what I am afraid you have done. You have treated God like a man who you can reason with and question. But God is not like humanity at all! He is free to contradict all our notions of Himself. He is mysterious in all His ways. The scriptures tell us that His ways are higher than our ways. It may be hard to swallow the Holocaust as God's will, but this fact remains true in the light of every other argument you can make because God is God and God is sovereign. We are not worthy to question Him.

Friedrich, I respect your position but fear I cannot say much more about it to you. You seem set in your ways. I have already said as much as I can tell you. God is free to do whatever He wants, and therefore our concepts of ethics and moralism are completely un-fitting in this discussion. It matters not what we find ethical. What matters is the sovereign will of God and the plan He has for humanity. This plan remains right even if we cannot see it. There's not much more I can say about that beyond what has already been said by myself or Clive (as I do agree with his concise argument against atheism, and I find your rebuttal sloppy).

Jurgen: Well then gentlemen, this has been entertaining. I've got to run to my lecture now. Who's got the bill this week? I believe it's Jean's turn, correct? If I recall, Friedrich picked it up last time which makes today Jean's responsibility and next week mine.

Jean: You're right, I'd forgotten about the bill. This has been captivating everyone, I'm looking forward to next week! And Clive, do let me know when you've finished Dostoyevsky. I'd love to see what you think of the rest of it!

Clive: Thanks, I will!

Friedrich: Good-bye! See you all next week.

2

JURGEN'S CRITIQUE

Friedrich: Jurgen, before we begin today with your critique, I'd like to share a great quote I read this week. Since we're talking about the Holocaust, I went ahead and picked up Night. What a gripping book it was! E. Wiesel, an Auschwitz survivor, tells the horrific details of his experience in the camp. I'll read a passage that was particularly powerful:

> Never shall I forget that night, the first night in
>   camp, that turned my life into a long night
>   seven times sealed.
> Never shall I forget that smoke.
> Never shall I forget the small faces of the
>   children whose bodies I saw transformed
>   into smoke under a silent sky.
> Never shall I forget those flames that consumed
>   my faith forever.
> Never shall I forget the nocturnal silence that
>   deprived me for all eternity of the desire
>   to live.

> Never shall I forget those moments that
>   murdered my God and my soul and my
>   dreams to ashes.
> Never shall I forget those things, even where I
>   condemned to live as long as 'God Himself.
> Never.
>
>   — NIGHT, 34

Clive: "...under a silent sky." Wow, that is profound, Friedrich. Great quote, and thank you for presenting it to us.

Friedrich: I might have guessed you'd enjoy the subtlety of that line, Clive. It's incredibly profound. The whole book is. I was deeply stirred while reading it. I finished the entire book in one sitting.

Jean: I remember reading it at university. It's a compelling book.

Jurgen: Yes, I would agree; I've read it as well. *Night* is an excellent book. But should we begin?

Friedrich: Right, yes of course. So I believe we left last time having stated our initial arguments and counter-arguments. I presented an atheistic answer to our dilemma, Jean presented a determinist position, and Clive presented a defense against both and an appeal to mystery. Is that a fair characterization you two?

Clive: Sounds fair to me.

Jean: I'm not fond of being labeled a determinist, let's stick to a more classical characterization. My position comes from Calvin, so we could call it the Calvinist position. I'd like that much better.

Friedrich: Fair enough, Jean.

Alright then Jurgen, seeing that this is your field of study, let's hear what you think. You did promise a critique today.

Jurgen: Yes, I didn't forget. And my critique is fairly simple, though it may take some explaining. Overall, what I found in listening last week is that each of you are faulted for the same mistake. As I sat and thought it through this became even clearer. You all may see errors in each others reasoning, but from my perspective, you are all still reasoning from within the same problematic framework. This common error you share is known to men and women in my field as natural theology. Now it's not a closed case; some argue that natural theology is not a problem at all. However, I disagree, and I will tell you why. But first, I'll define it for you so we are all on the same page. Natural theology is a mixture of philosophy and theology which attempts to prove either God's existence or to define God's nature with the use of human reasoning or observations of the natural world. Hence the name "natural" theology. It is, in a sense, working from our world up into God, reasoning from the finite to the Infinite. This framework of thought is the same for each of your positions, and I am convinced that it is an erroneous method to answer the question of God. The great 20th-century theologian Karl Barth famously argued against natural theology, although he also had (and still has) his opponents.

Clive: I'm sorry to cut in, but what's wrong with human reasoning? Isn't that all we have to begin with?

Friedrich: Yes, and how am I guilty of natural theology? I don't have any sort of theology at all. It's definitely not fair to say that I've performed something rooted in what I don't believe in.

Jurgen: Well, okay gentlemen. Hold on just a moment. I suppose if I back up some we can make this clearer. I'll take each position one at a time. What I'm talking about here is a method used to deduce theological ideas. And yes, even Atheism is a theology, Friedrich. Theology is "God knowledge." Even if you believe there is no God, that's still a kind of knowledge you have about God. This knowledge just happens to tell you that God is not real, but negative knowledge is still knowledge. What I mean to say in this critique is that the conclusions of your respective deductions are flawed because of the mutual method used to deduce them.

Friedrich, you've come to the conclusion that there is no rational belief in God post-Holocaust. But why? Your method of deduction is that a) since the event happened, b) God must not exist. But how did you work your way up from A into B? The conclusion was drawn because you took what you could observe in history and you lifted that up into God (since evil exists, God must not), but that's a flawed way of thinking. God is not the world; God is not finite. Therefore, any

observations made of a finite world cannot be used to mold the defini-
tion of an infinite God. The finite cannot speak of the Infinite. So I
ask again: how can the existence of the Holocaust have anything at all
to say about the existence of God?

Friedrich: But that's not entirely fair Jurgen. I'm not saying that
since the world is evil, God cannot exist. I'm instead saying that if God
exists, God must be good. Therefore, since the Holocaust exist, this
fact clashes with the fact that God is good. And thus, since I can prove
to you the existence of evil, but not the existence of God, I must reject
God in the light of evil. In my mind, that starts with God. So what's
the problem with that, Jurgen?

Jurgen: Who told you that God is good? Why must God be good
is God exists? From where did you get that idea, Friedrich? I'm not
trying to say that God isn't good, but the fact that you make this claim
makes me wonder where you got that idea in the first place. Could it
be that even there, in your assertion that "if God exists He must be
good", you have fallen into natural theology?

Friedrich: I'm not sure I follow you. How did you come to that
conclusion?

Jurgen: Well here is what I think you are doing, whether you know
it or not. I believe you've based your reasoning on Greek philosophy,
which theorizes the nature of God in abstract terms. You assume that
God is good if God is real, but where did you get that idea? The
Greeks got it from humanity. They proposed that since God is the
"ultimate" of humanity, that is since God is the end of our collaborate
pursuits, then God must be the perfect idea of man. The Greek philosophy of Plato and Aristotle is notorious for taking human attributes
and amplifying them to the nth degree. In this way, natural theology
creates a God in the image of man. The old saying goes that "God
created man in His image, and man has returned the favor ever since."
That is the method I am talking about. You discuss a God who is
"good," but where did you get that idea? From humanity! You have
followed the Greeks in taking that which is admirable in humanity,
and you have then perfected those attributes by plastering them onto
the face of God. You have spoken of God "by speaking of man in a

loud voice" (Barth). In this way, your God cannot be a God who exists because if you were God, you would not let the Holocaust happen. Therefore, at the very root of your argument, you have practiced natural theology.

Since you cannot imagine a God who is not like you, in your vision of God, deduced from humanity, God wouldn't allow the Holocaust to happen. Therefore, since it has happened, you reject the very same God you have created in your own image. You have taken a finite understanding of goodness, as interpreted by you, and you have defined God by it in order to reject God altogether. But you cannot know God like this, Friedrich. God is not like us, God is God. We must understand our conclusions in the light of who God reveals Himself to be, not in the light of what we perceive Him to be like in our finite understanding.

Clive: What exactly are you saying, Jurgen? Do you mean to say that it's impossible to know God? What's the point of theology then?

Jurgen: Theology is purely an act of grace. We can only know God by the grace of God. In our finite existence it is impossible to know God, but through grace God reveals Himself. Just as we cannot find salvation through our self- striving and efforts, we cannot deduce knowledge of God through self-striving and efforts! You know that well, Clive. Salvation is by grace through faith, but so is the knowledge of God. We know God only through God Himself.

Jean: I see what you're saying, Jurgen, and I agree! It reminds me of what Jesus said in Matthew 11:27, "No one knows the Son except the Father, and no one knows the Father except the Son and anyone to whom the Son chooses to reveal him." Jesus is clearly saying that God reveals Himself only to the elect. You're talking about the doctrine of election! But how does my position fall into this same error? I can see how Friedrich is at fault of Natural theology, but I'm not sure I see how I am.

Jurgen: Well, you make your conclusions in a similar way, do you not? While your concept of God is different than Friedrich's, this is the only difference between your position and his. In your doctrine of God the sovereign will of God is supreme, whereas, in Friedrich's, God goodness is supreme. You understand very well the fact that God is God, as you said last week, and this leads to your doctrine of God that opposes Greek philosophy. However, you are still stuck within your determinist framework. I know you dislike the term, but I believe it's your fundamental flaw. You can't shake this inherent determinism in your doctrine of predestination which influences your understanding of the sovereignty of God. In this framework, you still practice natural theology just as Friedrich has. Your conclusion is that the Holocaust must be in the will of God since it happened in a world where God is sovereign. But what if you've misunderstood sovereignty? I believe you have, friend. Where did you get this determinist doctrine of sovereignty anyways? In my observation, this seems to be very similar to how a deist might understand sovereignty. You're working with a Newtonian framework, which can only understand the world as a series of mechanistic events. It's as if God is a divine clockmaker, and our world events are predetermined as the gears and pulleys of His system. To this deist God, the Holocaust is just another event in the greater cosmic plan. Therefore, you must conclude that the Holocaust is God's will or your whole system falls apart. Your framework necessitates your conclusion. Within this framework, you are forced to work in the flaw of natural theology. You deduce that since the Holocaust happened, God must have made it happen because God is sovereign in a determinist sort of way. This, in turn, leads to the assertion that God caused, willed, and took delight in the happening of this event. Friedrich is very right in his critique! Your God is a monster. Your God smiled upon the slaughter of eleven million human beings!

But at the same time, I understand where you are coming from my friend. You have to answer in this way according to your predetermined framework of hyper-sovereignty. Your understanding of this world event as an event which speaks of God is flawed, and if you think through your assertion that "God is God" far enough, you will see this as well. God is God, you are correct! And therefore, God is free to be separate from our world events. He is not the cause of these events nor does He takes delight in these events. God is defined by God alone, and not by the events of our finite world. Remember, as I said to Friedrich, the fundamental flaw is that you attempt to speak of the Infinite with the finite. It cannot be done! The Holocaust, as a finite event, cannot speak of God in His infinite nature. The finite cannot know the Infinite, speak of the Infinite, or project even the most logical of deductions onto the Infinite. You've created a causal relationship between a finite event and an infinite God, but such causality cannot exist. Does this make sense to you, Jean?

Jean: Theoretically Jurgen, I suppose you may be onto something. But what are you saying? Are you trying to argue that God is not sovereign? I doubt you are, so then tell me: how can a sovereign God not be a God who is in control of all world events? I'm afraid you might need a refresher on the doctrine of sovereignty. I recommend you take a look again at Isaiah 46:10, Psalms 135:6, Job 42:2, and 1 Chronicles 29:12.

Jurgen: Don't worry Jean, I am not trying to pull a fast one on you. I am a firm believer in the sovereignty of God; I just wouldn't equate sovereignty with determinism! This is my quarrel with you. I do believe in sovereignty, but not in the way you have understood sovereignty as ultimate "control." It's a conversation I'm willing to have with you at a later date, Jean. If you'd like we can "compare notes," so to speak, on the subject, but for now I think it's best we stick to the dilemma at hand. Sovereignty as control or no sovereignty at all, the point still stands that your deduction follows the same methodology of natural theology. You conclude that God caused the Holocaust because the Holocaust takes place in a world made by an all-powerful God. The fact that the event has happened makes you conclude that God caused it to happen. Thus, you work from the finite world to the Infinite nature of God, i.e., natural theology.

Jean: Fair enough, Jurgen. I'll take the bait for now. But I'd still like to have that sovereignty conversation eventually.

Jurgen: Certainly, I plan on it, but let me unveil my position first, okay? Once you see that perhaps you may also see how I understand sovereignty in the light of our current theodicy dilemma.

Clive: I'm next then, correct? But I'm afraid I don't see how your natural theology critique poses any problem for my position. And even if it did, I'm still not convinced that natural theology is all that bad. I mean, didn't God give us reasoning for a purpose? Why would revelation contradict logic? If God is the God of both, how is it fair to say that one is an error while another is not?

Jurgen: You're right, Clive, your position doesn't necessarily follow the same methodology, but I also wouldn't say that your view classically could be defined as theodicy at all. You don't answer the original dilemma; you merely say what you don't believe. So, of course, the natural theology critique doesn't fit. You never really say anything about our dilemma; you merely defend the nature of God in spite of the Holocaust. It's a noble thing to do, I must say, but it's not what we're doing here. So my critique is different for you.

Clive: Okay Jurgen, that's fair. I suppose you're free to break your own rules if I'm guilty of violating them too. So let's hear it.

Jurgen: Well to start I must tell you that I think your response it the best of the bunch, but I also must be honest at the same time. So while I found your reasoning to be spot on, and your conclusion well presented, the implications of your deductions are perhaps the worst of all. You have left us with nothing to truly say in the face of the Holocaust. It's my firm conviction that theology must not be done in abstraction from humanity or else it becomes inhuman. Theology must be willing and able to stand face to face with the tragedies of humanity and give an answer to them. A theology which fails to do just that is an inhuman, impractical theology of no worth to anyone. So that's my first strike against your position, Clive. You present an abstract, heartless theology. You fail to answer any of the questions at all. Instead, you work around the questions and leave them unanswerable.

Now, I am not one to claim that theology has to have all the answer to all of the questions, so I do respect your appeal to unknowing. But in the face of such serious dilemmas, I believe theology must have something to say. Karl Barth famously said of liberal theology that it left him with nothing to preach. I'm afraid this may be your discovery as well. While your theory sounds nice, it leaves us with nothing to go on. It certainly gets God off the hook, but it fails on all accounts to answer the theodicy question at all.

You answer well the question of whether or not God caused the Holocaust, but you fail to answer where God was in the Holocaust.

And that is our present dilemma. It matters theoretically perhaps to know whether or not God caused the Holocaust, and I do believe you are right in your assertion that He does not. However, for those who are suffering and for those who have suffered in the past the question is not "who is to blame?", the question is, "where is God?" Jean has answered that God wills and therefore takes part in the Holocaust event, and Friedrich argues that God was not there because there is no God. However, you have essentially claimed unknowability to get yourself off the hook. You have therefore failed to answer the question at hand, the one which matters—the one cried out in the hearts of every victim of suffering: Where is God?

The second problem I have with your answer, I'm afraid, is far worse. The implications of your thought may lead an individual to conclude that this God you are defending is an indifferent God. You say you don't know where God was in the Holocaust, and I'm afraid the only direction that sort of thinking can lead to is to eventually conclude that God is indifferent to the suffering of humanity. The indifference of God is the worst possible position you could take because indifference is the opposite of love. If God is a God of love, He cannot be an indifferent God. The wrath of God, as difficult a subject as it is, still points to a God of love. At least a God of wrath is a God who cares. An indifferent God can neither love nor hate, and therefore condemns humanity to an eternity of indifference. There is no horror greater than that of an indifferent God! I know this is never a conclusion you would make, but for those who hear your position, this is a logical necessity. Since you cannot answer where God was in the Holocaust, God must be indifferent to suffering (some might say). You may never say it, but it is implied in your thought. That, Clive, is the critique I offer for your position.

I found your deductions to be wholly un-theological. In defending God, you failed to say anything of God or to take the revelation of God in Jesus Christ seriously. Therefore, you may be half right, but being half right is still being wrong.

But enough of that, let me speak to you all more generally. I hope I haven't thrown you all off guard with my criticisms. Let me be as clear as I can in laying out my position for you. The essential critique is that the finite cannot know the Infinite. This is an axiom that I hope you can see as true. God must then reveal Himself if we are to know God. This remains true in the question of the Holocaust. If we are to know where God was in the Holocaust, we must deduce that knowledge from God Himself. We must then propose the question more like this: In revelation, where was God in the Holocaust? What has God revealed about Himself in suffering? Since only God can reveal God, only God can answer our original question. The table must be cleared of all philosophical deductions which do not begin with God Himself. Any concept of God which derives from natural theology must be thrown out. It's not that reasoning fails to be consistent with revelation. Instead, logic must work within revelation rather than outside of it.

Jean: Well, those are some interesting ideas you have there Jurgen. I'd love to know what your position is; it's interesting enough to find out what it isn't! Seeing that we're nearly out of time, will you be able to present it to us next week?

Jurgen: Actually, I have a proposal for you all. What if you sat in on my lecture this Thursday? It so happens that this week I am presenting my answer to the theodicy question as a part of my Christology class. I'll be lecturing Thursday afternoon from 2:45 until 4.

Clive: That sounds like a great idea. I've never heard you lecture before Jurgen, but I've heard it's a delight!

Jean: Yes, count me in. That sounds like a good time. I'll be grading papers all day Thursday anyways; it'll be a nice little break for me to come and listen.

Jurgen: Excellent. And you Friedrich? Can you make it?

Friedrich: Unfortunately I have a class starting at three that day. But I feel my contribution to this conversation may be running thin anyways. I'm still set in my atheism, whether or not it's the by-product of natural theology, and so I don't see how debating further will do any good.

Jurgen: I understand, but can I make a recommendation? It's worth considering Anselm's ontological argument for God. I don't know if you've heard of him or not before, but his ontological argument for God's existence is, in my opinion, one of the best. It's worth looking into if you have the time.

Friedrich: No, I haven't heard of Anselm before, but I'll look him up. Thanks.

Jurgen: No problem. Now I'm afraid I've got to run off and teach a class. Good-bye! I'll see you two on Thursday.

Clive: I'm looking forward to it!

3

CHRISTOLOGY 101

Clive and Jean sit down in the back of Jurgen's classroom as he begins to lecture.

"Where is God in human suffering?" Today we will examine theodicy in the light of Jesus Christ. As we've discussed in previous lectures, all theology must be Christology. Therefore, we must "begin again" with the person of Jesus Christ as the one revelation of God revealed in scripture.

Now, will someone read out loud page 140 from your theology textbooks? Read paragraphs sixteen and seventeen only, please. Yes, you, thank you.

> Its problems accordingly resulted from the fact that the Father of Jesus Christ was identified with the one God of Greek metaphysics and had the attributes of this God ascribed to him.
>
> — MOLTMANN: THEOLOGY OF HOPE, 140-1

Hold on a moment before you continue, Steve. Could anyone tell me who the "it" in this sentence is referring to? If you remember our last class, this should be apparent.

"The early church?"

Yes, thank you. The author here is discussing the early church's initial clash with Greek metaphysics. You may continue reading.

> The God who reveals himself in Jesus must be thought of as the God of the Old Testament, as the God of the exodus and the promise, as the God 'with future as his essential nature', and therefore must not be identified with the Greek view of God, with Parmenides' 'eternal present' of Being, with Plato's highest Idea and with the Unmoved Mover of Aristotle, not even in his attributes. Who he is, is not declared by the world as a whole, but is declared by Israel's history of promise [...] Christian theology has to think along this line. It is not that a general truth became concrete in Jesus, but the concrete, unique, historic event of the crucifying and raising of Jesus by Yahweh, the God of promise who creates being out of nothing, becomes general through the universal eschatological horizon it anticipates. Through the raising of Jesus from the dead the God of the promises of Israel becomes the God of all men.
>
> — IBID., 141-42

Good, thank you. Now, class, on the board I have drawn two triangles. The first is upside down with the large end at the top, and the second is right side up with the small pointed end at the top. These two triangles represent what the author is saying are the two methodologies possible in theology. On the one hand we have the universal to the particular or the first triangle; on the other hand, we have the particular to the universal, or the second triangle.

The Greek philosophy of Plato and Aristotle is the best example of the first triangle. The Greeks began their theology from general concepts of God. Plato specifically was concerned with God as the end of man's ultimate concern, as the "highest good" of humanity. Therefore, this leads to an understanding of God as ultimate and abstract.

Examining the second triangle, you can see the Christological method of theology which works in contrast to the Greeks. This deals exclusively and particularly with the one revelation of Jesus Christ, and accomplishes this revelation out into the general and universal.

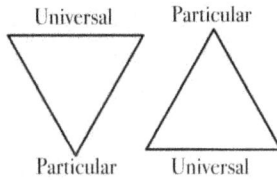

Universal   Particular

Particular   Universal

In the first method, that of Greek philosophy, God is thought of in abstract terms and then these notions are attributed to the particular person of Jesus Christ. Therefore, Jesus Christ becomes divorced from the history and individuality of the Jewish people. In a sense, the Greek method of theology turns Jesus Christ into a non-historical, transcendental figure.

In the second method, however, the history and culture of Israel are taken far more seriously. God is thought of as the particular God of the Jewish people, the God of Abraham, Isaac, and Jacob. This God reveals Himself in Jesus Christ, in the universal death of Christ, as the God of all humanity. Thus the Apostle Paul writes that "there is neither Jew nor Greek, there is neither slave nor free, there is no male and female, for you are all one in Christ Jesus" (Galatians 3:28, ESV). The particular Jewish God of Israel has become the God of all humanity in Jesus Christ.

These two methods are in sharp contrast with one another. One cannot work from a general, abstract, platonic concept of God and attribute those concepts to the person of Jesus Christ. Instead, theology must begin with Jesus Christ. A theology which begins anywhere else is a failure from the start. Jesus Christ alone is the particular God of Israel in the flesh who has become the universal God of all humanity. Now, throughout the history of the church, particularly the history of the western church, it's common to practice this method of Greek philosophy. Due to the influence of Thomas Aquinas and Augustine, this platonic method of generalizations applied to Jesus Christ has significantly influenced theology as we know it today. To ask, "who is God?" in today's world is to hear the response "God is omnipotent, omnipresent, omnibenevolent, impassible, and immutable." But where did all these concepts come from? We could say that they are found in the person of Jesus Christ, but what if they were applied to Him? What if our common notions of God have been deduced not from the particular revelation of Jesus Christ, but from the general philosophy of Plato and Aristotle? The theories of an "unmoved mover" and "loveless beloved" are dominant in Christian theology in the aftermath of Greek metaphysics, but if these notions are deduced from philosophy rather than theology—for theology has to begin only with Jesus Christ as the revelation of God—then we must rethink our theology altogether. We must begin again with the God revealed in Jesus Christ.

In short, we have to follow the outline of this second triangle. We must begin with Jesus Christ who becomes the universal God, rather than to begin with a general, abstract God and to apply this God to the person of Christ then. This method also includes our present question. We have discussed at length the ramifications of a post-Barthian theology, and the undeniable truth that God can only reveal Godself. Today we will continue in this Christological focus by answering the difficult question of "where is God in human suffering?" As I have shown, we must begin with the person of Jesus Christ as the particular God who becomes universal. Therefore any abstract notions of God will not work in this discussion. We have to deal with the particular person of Jesus Christ: Where has Jesus suffered? Where was God in that suffering? How can theodicy find a solution in the life of Jesus Christ?

A popular claim among some of my colleagues is the now infamous declaration, "God is dead." While it's important to negate this claim with the fact that God is not dead, we cannot fall into the reactionary error of saying that God cannot die, for in the person of Jesus Christ God did die. God is not dead, but God has died at a particular time and place in history. If any of you hear this voice in your head saying, "but God can't die!" please silence it immediately. This is your inherent

Greek philosophy trying to limit what God can and cannot do. Just remember what we've said. God is not the general God of Platonic philosophy applied to the particular person of Jesus Christ. God is Jesus Christ and Jesus Christ is God. Whatever your philosophy tells you, Jesus Christ is the first and final word of God. Since Jesus Christ as God has suffered and died, we must say that this is true of God Himself. "God cannot die" is an assertion refuted by the cross of Jesus Christ.

Paul Althaus has said that "Christology must be done in the light of the cross: the full and undiminished deity of God is to be found in the complete helplessness, in the final agony of the crucified Jesus" (cited in Moltmann: *The Crucified God*, 206). If we are to "begin again" with Jesus Christ we must begin again with Jesus Christ as the crucified God. We must say in the light of the cross that God has died, and that as a result there is now death in God.

As an individual, the death of Jesus Christ is a death like others, but as God, as a Trinitarian God, Jesus Christ represents a striking change to our concept of God. If Jesus Christ truly is God in the flesh, then not only can God die, but there is death in the very Godhead Itself. The Trinitarian life of God is now centered around the suffering and death of the Son of the Father in the love of the Holy Spirit.

Now, before we develop this idea further, let me address a few of the counter-arguments which seem to negate it. I am here claiming that 1) since Jesus Christ suffered and died, God can suffer and die. And, 2) that, when this is worked out in a Trinitarian way, there is death in God.

The first argument is less of an argument per se, but it represents a significant reason why I feel most reject this claim. If one is to only interpret the cross as a soteriological event, that is, as a saving event, then such an individual sees this death as a means to an end. They fail however to take the theological ramifications of the death of Jesus Christ seriously. If understood by strict soteriology rather than theology, the cross does not imply a change in the doctrine of God. But if we take seriously the fact that Jesus Christ is the revelation of God, we cannot say anything else. The cross must influence our theology about

God, for the cross is essential to the whole gospel including our knowledge of God.

Another argument claims that since Jesus died on the cross, Jesus died only as a man and not as God and man. This takes the hypostatic union and splits it up into compartments. Some claim that since God "cannot" suffer or die in their doctrine of God, Jesus must cease to be God on the cross. This argument comes from Cyril of Alexandria. However, it fails to take seriously the hypostatic union. The union of God and man in the person of Jesus Christ is essential. We cannot take the life of Jesus and plot it on a chart separating which events are "divine" events and which are human. Jesus Christ is the God-man from birth to death to resurrection and ascension. To separate the person of Jesus Christ in order to justify your personal presupposition is a horrendous error to make, and it is wholly unethical. One cannot impose upon Jesus Christ any limitations on account of preconceived notions. If theology is to be done properly it must be done in the light of Jesus Christ, not behind His back. To take the person of Jesus Christ seriously is to recognize the fact that, as Paul writes, "God was in Christ." This too is the best stance against this argument. There is no scriptural evidence to imply that Jesus Christ was only a human being on the cross. God was in Christ, and therefore God suffered and died on that cross with Jesus Christ.

Now, with these arguments out of the way, let's continue to develop this position. If God was in Christ, then we must say that it is this God who is in our human suffering as well. Simply, the answer to our original question is found here. Where is God in human suffering? God is in human suffering! God has met us in the thick of our pain and calamity and even in our death. God is with us in all things: in all joy, in all sorrow, and in all the mundaneness of life. On the cross this becomes clear. God joins us in our human suffering and even in our death. The theological conclusion of all this must then be, in the light of the cross, that God is affected by humanity. When we suffer, God suffers with us. When we die, God dies in our death.

> There is no suffering which in this history of God is not God's
> suffering; no death which has not been God's death in the history on

Golgotha. Therefore there is no life, no fortune and no joy which have not been integrated by his history into eternal life, the eternal joy of God.

— THE CRUCIFIED GOD, 246

In this way, we develop our theodicy even further. We must say in the light of the cross that God is in our suffering, feeling and being affected by our suffering, but we must also take it a step further and say that suffering is in God. History is in God, in fact. The truth is not only that God is in our human suffering, but that our human suffering is in God. The cross again is where this claim originates. God suffers in the suffering of Jesus Christ, and the suffering of Jesus Christ reaches into the suffering of the Trinity. As a Being of agape, of self-giving love, the self-sacrificial act of Jesus Christ is essential to the very being of God. Jesus Christ suffers and dies on the cross because this is what a God of love is like. A God who loves the world suffers with the world and takes our human sufferings upon Himself as His own sufferings. If God truly is love, and if the cross truly is the suffering of God, we can make no other claim than this.

On a side note, we mustn't say that this equates to patripassianism: that the Father died on the cross with the Son. Instead, we must assume that while Jesus alone is the incarnate one, the one who suffered and died in our flesh on the cross, the Trinity does not remain cold and distant from that event. Instead, while Jesus remains the one who practically suffers and dies, the Father and the Spirit are equally affected by His death. Think about it relationally, since God as a Trinity is a relational Being. The eternal love of God as the Father, Son, and Holy Spirit cannot remain indifferent to the suffering and death of the Son. What sort of Father would see the death of His Son and remain unaffected by it? We must speak in a Trinitarian way as we say that the death of Jesus Christ is also the grief of the Father and the suffering of the Spirit. The Father has given up the Son for the sake of humanity; this is the sacrifice of the Father. The Son is the recipient of suffering and death for the sake of atonement, but the Father and the Spirit are participants in that suffering in that they are affected by that

suffering. Therefore, it can be said that God is a suffering God. In the
heart of the Trinity is the death of Jesus Christ, the suffering grief of
the Father, and the horrific loss of the Spirit. So then, to make our
original question more Trinitarian, let's ask, "Where is the Trinity in
our human sufferings?" The answer can only come as we examine the
cross. The Son meets us in our suffering and death, the Father meets us
in our grief and sorrow, and the Spirit meets us in our rejection and
fear. The Son is with us in our suffering, and the Father and Spirit are
affected by our suffering. God takes humanity so seriously that He
makes Himself vulnerable to be affected by his sufferings. As C.S.
Lewis so wonderfully claimed: "to love at all is to be vulnerable." This
is especially true in the event of God on the cross. In our human
suffering, God makes Himself vulnerable to our history, taking our
history upon Himself as His own. God is therefore deeply affected by
our existence.

In our textbooks we read:

> Suffering is overcome by suffering, and wounds are healed by
> wounds. For the suffering in suffering is the lack of love, and the
> wounds in wounds are the abandonment, and the powerlessness in
> pain is unbelief. And therefore the suffering of abandonment is
> overcome by the suffering of love, which is not afraid of what is sick
> and ugly, but accepts it and takes it to itself in order to heal it.
> Through his own abandonment by God, the crucified Christ brings
> God to those who abandoned by God. Through his suffering he
> brings salvation to those who suffer. Through his death he brings
> eternal life to those who are dying.
>
> — MOLTMANN: THE CRUCIFIED GOD, 46

Before we conclude our Christological approach to theodicy, we
must take it one step further still. To say that God only meets us and is
affected by our suffering is not enough. God must also undo our

suffering and heal our pain; He must meet us in our death in order to resurrect us to new life. In suffering in our suffering, God does not justify or glorify suffering. Instead, God suffers for the sake of undoing suffering. God meets us in our darkness in order to shine the light of His love. God meets us in our pain in order to make us whole. Paradoxically, the power of God undoes the power of sin and death through the self-sacrificial love of Jesus Christ dying on the cross. Bonhoeffer wrote from prison, "Christ helps us, not by virtue of his omnipotence, but by virtue of his weakness and suffering [...] Only the suffering God can help" (*Letters and Papers from Prison,* 361).

The Gospel of Jesus Christ reveals the startling fact that God is not like the Gods and Goddesses of Greek mythology. God is not an inhuman God; God is the God of humanity. He is the God of Abraham, Isaac, and Jacob. He is our God, and He is for us. He is the suffering God because we are a suffering people and He has joined Himself to us. The gospel proclaims that God has met us in our sufferings. God has found us in the darkness of our abandonment and rejection and despair and He has healed us and included us in Himself. All our humanity is felt from within God's very self because He has taken our humanity upon Himself. All of it, both the good and the bad, is now history in God's existence. God participates both in our human victories of courage and valor and in our human sorrows of pain and suffering.

Additionally, if we take this one step further still, we develop an important, new dynamic for soteriology. For most, the Gospel message proclaims salvation to offenders. The Gospel claims that God can forgive anyone. If you murder, commit sin after sin, and come to God repentant and humble you can be forgiven. This is the outrageous grace of God! But what of the victims of sin? What about those who have suffered at the hands of sinners? What of those murdered by the murderers? What of those raped? A Christian Gospel which offers only healing for the offenders is a Gospel missing half its content. The Gospel of Jesus Christ justifies both the sinner and the victim. Jesus, as a man who suffers unjustly, justified both the Roman guards who drove the nails into His hands and the fellow sufferer who cried out to Him from the other cross. Both must be reached by the Gospel if the

Gospel is to be good news. God is not only for the sinners and the oppressors; God is for their victims too. What we've been discussing here leads to a profound theodicy, but it also brings about a more robust soteriology.

Now, in closing our discussion today, let's briefly review what we've covered.

Proper theology works within the methodology of the second triangle on the board, the right side up triangle. It works from the particular history of Israel and the God revealed in Jesus Christ towards the general God of all humanity. We cannot begin with the general and abstract and then work our way to Jesus Christ. We must always be willing to "begin again" with Jesus Christ as the God of Israel who becomes the God of all humanity.

Therefore, whenever we ask, "where is God in human suffering?", the only truly theological answer is: "God was in Christ" (2 Cor. 5:19). Jesus Christ suffers and dies as God, and therefore there is death in God. To say that God cannot die is to repeat the error spoken of above. This Greek notion is expelled

in the light of Jesus Christ. The Crucified Christ is thus the answer to the theodicy dilemma. On the cross, Jesus Christ suffers and dies, and therefore we must conclude that in our suffering and death God has reached us, joining us then and there. God takes humanity so seriously as to be affected by our suffering. God has met us in our suffering, and our suffering has been taken up into the life of God. The Cross stands in the heart of the Trinity as the death of the Son and the suffering of His Father. Therefore, God is the Crucified God who suffers with humanity and who takes our sufferings upon Himself.

And finally, the suffering of God is healing to our human suffering. God not only suffers in our suffering, taking it upon Himself, but God also heals and undoes our suffering with His suffering. As Bonhoeffer wrote, "only the suffering God can help." A God who cannot suffer with the sufferings of humanity is an inhuman God who has left us hopeless in our darkness. The God revealed in Jesus Christ is the God who undoes suffering by meeting us in our suffering and taking our suffering upon Himself.

So class, where is God in our human suffering? He is right here, with us, suffering and dying there on the cross, in our sufferings, and in our deaths.

For homework, keep working on your essays on the two great patristic works of Christology: Athanasius' On the Incarnation and Irenaeus' Against Heresies (Book III). These are due next week! Fifteen pages, single-spaced, and nothing bigger than twelve point font. Make sure you're citing your sources, too. Class dismissed. Have a great afternoon everyone, see you next week.

4

DISCUSSING CLASSICS

Okay reader, I have a confession to make. I need to unceremoniously "kill off" Friedrich from this conversation if we're going to get serious about it. It's not that I don't like Friedrich, I'm sure if he was a real person he'd be a lot of fun, but that's just the thing, this is a fictional conversation, not a real one. The primary subject at hand is theology, and so I have to eventually get around to the point, which is hard to do with Friedrich's constant atheism barking down our backs. That's not the problem this book is trying to solve. This isn't an apologetic book about the existence of God. Like Jurgen said in chapter two, Anselm's ontological argument is all I have to plead in regards to that debate. So let that be the music we play him off to. Friedrich is no longer a part of this discussion, come up with whatever reason you'd like. Perhaps his in-laws are in town, and he can't get away, or maybe he just lost interest. Either way, Friedrich is gone for the sake of us getting to the real point of this book. Let's continue then.

Jurgen: Alright, so what did you think?

Clive: I found it enjoyable, Jurgen, it was a pleasure to hear you in your element!

Jurgen: Thank you!

Jean: Yea, I would agree. Well done! Jurgen: I'm glad you enjoyed it.

Clive: An interesting exercise I like to do before each of my lectures is to summarize what I want to say in a sentence. That way I'll know if I can't be concise, what I have to say probably won't stick... or at least that's what I've found. Have you ever tried this?

Jurgen: I haven't, but maybe I could come up with a quick summary now. Let me think... Well, I suppose I could put it like this: God is like Jesus Christ dying on the cross; what He has done there He has done in all times and all places.

Jean: Maybe I was in the wrong lecture, Jurgen, but that's not what I would have said. How did you come up with that?

Jurgen: Well, I suppose it's more about how I concluded what I said; the whole lecture is built on that foundation. I'll break it down for you. Our question was theodicy, correct? So we began by asking "who is God?", because theodicy must begin there. I brought up this point a lot in our critiques. Your framework is dictated by your image of God, so we have to start there. Who is God? God is Jesus Christ hanging on a cross. God cannot be any other God than this God. God cannot be hypothesized as some abstract Greek deity, or as one or many of the philosophical concepts of God. God is exclusive. That was what the whole triangle business was about. God is Jesus Christ, the tip of the pyramid. We cannot work it out the other way around. We begin with one particular man, the God-man Jesus Christ, who belongs to a particular time, within a particular event. All these particularities become universal as well, but they begin with particular facts. The phrase I kept saying is that we must "begin again" with Jesus Christ. That comes from Karl Barth. You could probably sum up the entire Church Dogmatics along with the countless other volumes Barth has produced with the two words "Jesus Christ." For Barth, Jesus Christ is the answer to any theological question we can propose. As the old Barthian joke goes: "The answer is Jesus Christ, what's the question?" This is what I mean here with the particularity of theology.

We have to begin again with Jesus Christ alone as the revelation of God.

So that's the first part: God is like Jesus Christ. Now of course, I know God is Jesus Christ, but I'm afraid too many people simply skip over the epistemological ramifications of that fact. If Jesus is God, then God is like Jesus. Barth was particularly interested in removing any sort of God behind the back of Jesus Christ. There is no God hidden behind Jesus Christ; God is like Jesus.

Next, I became even more particular with the cross. The crucified Christ is the "image of the invisible God" Paul wrote about. This God is like this, like the crucified Christ.

> God is not greater than he is in humiliation. God is not more glorious than he is in this self-surrender. God is not more divine than he is in this humanity. The nucleus of everything that Christian theology says about 'God' is to be found in this Christ event. The Christ event on the cross is a God event. And conversely, the God event takes place on the cross of the risen Christ.
>
> — MOLTMANN: THE CRUCIFIED GOD, 205

And finally, the last part is where I practically work out this particular image of God into the universal question of theodicy. If this is what God is like, then in all times and in all places God is the suffering God who suffers in our suffering and who takes our sufferings upon Himself. Our history is in God, and God is in our history. However, this all begins with Jesus Christ, the crucified God. It is this God who is in our suffering and who takes our suffering upon Himself.

So there you have it. Any questions?

Clive: Well said; no questions here. I think your position is extremely beautiful. Although I'm not sure how this all reflects on God theologically. I mean, what about the impassibility of God? That's the doctrine that God cannot suffer, isn't it? I think you mentioned it in passing during your lecture, but what do you make of it? I've often wondered why theologians teach that God cannot suffer when Jesus Christ suffered and died Himself.

Jean: Yes, now that I think about it I'm curious too. And can I add to the list? That is if we're making one. I want to know what this also could mean for a few other doctrines like omnipotence and sovereignty. You did promise me that conversation eventually if you haven't forgotten.

Jurgen: Right you are Jean, I didn't forget. I'll add another to the list while we're at it. We should also discuss the immutability of God, which simply means God cannot change. It's a minor one, but still relevant in a theology centered on the crucified God.

Clive: Oh right, I always forget about that one.

Jurgen: I'm glad these have come up. It's telling me you two are thinking seriously about what I said. That's good. I think we should begin with Omnipotence; it's the easiest to explain from the list. Plus it's important to our discussion. If God is all-powerful, how can God let the Holocaust happen? That's our essential problem when we deal with theodicy. Either God is not all powerful, or God is not all good. That's the classical dead-lock that comes up in this sort of thinking, but I believe I can offer a solution here that may change the way we work out this issue.

But first, let's all get a round of coffee. It smells wonderful, and we may be here for a while.

Jurgen: I've found that the "problem" of omnipotence (in terms of theodicy) quickly goes away as soon as we get our framework right. In my lecture, I touched on something that we discussed some last week. It is an error to begin with Greek notions of God and work out a thesis from there. You'll often create an idol, theologically speaking, whenever you begin with anyone or anything other than Jesus Christ. So we've got to get our framework right by taking Jesus Christ seriously. And when do, the theodicy problem of an omnipotent, omnibenevolent God quickly becomes less of a dilemma.

In Corinthians 1:27 Paul writes: "God chose what is foolish in the world to shame the wise; God chose what is weak in the world to shame the strong; God chose what is low and despised in the world, even things that are not, to bring to nothing things that are." Here we discover a clue towards solving this dilemma. God's power is different than our power. The way we tend to understand power is like Superman. Superman personifies the absolute power that we might expect from an absolute God. He is Superman, our vision of power amplified to the nth degree. This, if you remember, is the conclusion of natural theology. However, Paul makes it clear by this statement that God's power is not power as we know it. Instead, power begins at the cross. If we want to know what the power of God looks like, not abstractly but practically, we must look only towards the death of Jesus Christ. Here we see God's victory over sin and darkness. Here, as Jesus Christ suffers and dies in weakness and humiliation, God flexes His divine muscles and solves our human corruption.

Therefore, the power of God is a paradox. God wins by losing. God brings about a new creation through death and suffering. This is what God is like. God remains all-powerful, but our understanding of power must be grounded in Jesus Christ the crucified Messiah. This loser out-casted from Jewish society turns out to be the winner of all human history. This paradox is the paradox of God's power. A Christocentric theology can make no other claim.

Jean: Well, sure that's an interesting perspective Jurgen. But what about the resurrection? That event certainly seems like the proper use of God's power! You can call it a "Superman" event if you'd like, but how does it play into your understanding of the Omnipotence of God? In my mind, the resurrection contradicts what you're saying here.

Jurgen: Ah yes, the resurrection! Could you imagine how this event would have taken place if either one of us were in charge of it? I'll tell you what; I bet you it would have been much different from the story we read in the Gospel accounts.

For starters, Jesus would have raised publicly. The resurrection would be the once-and-for-all proof that God exists! No more need for Apologetics or the God-debate. If we could raise Jesus Christ from the dead and make this fact clear to all humanity, then everyone would believe! I'm sure this would be how most of us would have done it. Jesus would have raised from the dead with fireworks and neon lights. But what actually took place? The accounts seem to tell us a much stranger story. Jesus raises from the dead in secret. His own disciples doubted that it happened right up until they could touch the scars on His body. If they even doubted it makes you wonder, what was God thinking? Didn't God miss an opportunity to show off His "power" for the whole world to undeniably see?

The resurrection event is just as paradoxical as the crucifixion. In some respects, it may be even more of an enigma! It was a left-handed act, not a right-handed magic trick. God works paradoxically in His omnipotence even at the resurrection. I mean, I think you're on to something, Jean, but consider the actual account itself. While it may seem like a grand spectacle to us 2,000 years away from it, it was anything but one. The Gospels tell that the first witnesses to this event were a group of women. Women! 2,000 years ago a woman's word was worthless. Why would God let the first witnesses to His grand magic trick be a group of women?

This fact points yet again to the left-handed paradoxical use of power. So no, I'm sorry Jean, but the resurrection cannot be used as a universal trump card like you'd hoped! God does not prove anything. He acts almost more mysteriously in the resurrection and ascension. It's all just strange if you ask my honest reflection. It does not seem like something Superman would do. But it does fit in quite well with the paradoxical power of the Crucified Christ.

Clive: I think you're right, Jurgen. I've never thought of the resurrection like that. I guess it's difficult to "un-Christianize" the whole event after 2,000 years of church history's attempt to turn it into a universal trump card. But you're right, it's all there in the gospels. There's nothing special about that event at all on the surface level. If anything, it's just another day for the world. Nobody besides a handful of ragamuffins were left with this odd story to proclaim to the rest of humanity.

Jurgen: You're right about that. History has a way of romanticizing the past. I've found this to be true in my own life as well as in my historical studies of the bible.

Jean: Okay, so let's say your right. What about the Holocaust? How does this reflect on our original dilemma? That's the whole point, isn't it?

Jurgen: Well it gives us some more room to breathe, for starters. We don't have the same deadlock of a Superman God who must save out of omnibenevolence. Instead, we have something much more robust and beautiful. When you think about it, theodicy is just too complicated of a question to solve with such simplistic answers. That's what I'm afraid dominates the spectrum. We want pat answers to help us categorize God, but He won't allow it. He's God after all. So there is no must for God. God mustn't do a thing. But as an all-good God, He does. The cross tells us this as well.

So I suppose that's what I'd say to the original dilemma. Like I said in my lecture: God overcomes suffering with suffering, He raises us to life by joining us in death. That's how God paradoxically makes sense of the Holocaust, too. He joins us in suffering with the promise—a mysterious promise to say the least! But a promise still—that on the other side He has overcome the world. The Holocaust is in God, and God is in the Holocaust. Somehow, in God's paradoxical power, this means that all our human suffering is overcome in God. God has defeated death by joining us in death. Jesus Christ has overcome sin by becoming sin (2 Cor. 5:21). I believe somewhere in this there is a silver lining of hope which lasts beyond suffering and pain. God is not only in our suffering, but by taking our suffering as His own, God overcomes it.

Clive: That is beautiful, Jurgen, and it makes me anticipate your next answer. I'd love to know what you make of God's impassibility? You seem to be saying that God can suffer? That God feels and is hurt by us?

Jurgen: Yes, this is exactly what I'm saying. Impassibility is the doctrine that God cannot suffer, feel emotion (or more properly be affected by emotion), or be wounded. It comes from a general understanding of God in the abstract. A God of otherness is. Therefore, a God removed and distant from the human race. This bears with it the inherent problem of moving dangerously too close to the deist camp. An impassable God tends to be an indifferent God who is both uninvolved and unaffected by human history.

Personally, I believe that God is passible, not impassible. I believe that the impassibility of God is a monstrosity, one which should be removed immediately from all our textbooks and sermons. An author I read recently went as far as to say that an impassible God is a demon, and I suppose I would say the same. It's a strong statement to make, but the ramifications of the doctrine of impassibility can only lead to that conclusion.

So I suggest we begin again with Jesus Christ. On the obvious level, Jesus Christ suffers and dies. He therefore feels and is affected by the human race. We've already discussed the Cyrilian solution to this problem, which says that Jesus only suffered as a man, but I've also refuted that solution. And so, with that out of the way, the overall conclusion becomes simple. We either take Jesus Christ seriously, or we fall back upon our Greek metaphysics which stand in contradiction to Jesus Christ. I motion for the former. If we take Jesus Christ seriously as the one revelation of God in our flesh, then we must say that God is like Jesus, and therefore, God can and does suffer.

On the other hand, we must take this claim a step further still. God not only is capable of suffering but on the cross, God had defined Himself as a suffering God. The God of Jesus is the crucified God who suffers with the human race. God knows firsthand grief and suffering and even death. God defines Himself in Christ by this suffering. God is the suffering God who takes humanity so seriously that He becomes our partner in suffering.

Another strong argument against the impassibility of God comes from Johns famous axiom: "God is love." If God is love then God feels and God risks. A feeling and risking God is a God who can suffer, and therefore a God of passibility. As C.S. Lewis beautifully said of love:

> To love at all is to be vulnerable. Love anything and your heart will be wrung and possibly broken. If you want to make sure of keeping it intact you must give it to no one, not even an animal. Wrap it carefully round with hobbies and little luxuries; avoid all entanglements. Lock it up safe in the casket or coffin of your selfishness. But in that casket, safe, dark, motionless, airless, it will change. It will not be broken; it will become unbreakable, impenetrable, irredeemable. To love is to be vulnerable.

— THE FOUR LOVES

C. S. Lewis did not intend for this statement to reflect upon God, but if he's right about love then we are justified in saying that God's love is like this. God loves and therefore God is vulnerable, making Himself capable of suffering with those who suffer and of being affected by those who cry out to Him. Agape love is self-sacrificial love, and this love is central to the existence of the Trinity. Therefore, if God truly loves us, then God also suffers with us.

> If God were in every respect incapable of suffering, he would also be incapable of love. He would at most be able to love himself, but no anything other than himself. But if he is capable of loving something other than himself, then he opens himself for the suffering which love for the other brings him, while still remaining master of the pain which is the consequence of his love. God does not suffer out of deficiency of being, like created beings. But he does suffer from his love, which is the overflowing superabundance of his being. And in this sense he can suffer.

> — Moltmann: Jesus Christ for Today's World, 45

If God is impassable, then God is not love. Love by nature necessitates suffering with the beloved; a lover is always open to be affected by their beloved. In simple terms, therefore, the impassibility of God goes against the cross, the love of God, and the Trinitarian life of God.

For a moment everyone is silent.

I'm sorry, it seems that I've overrun this conversation with my ramblings. My apologies. Does anyone else have something to add?

Jean: Don't be sorry Jurgen, it's obvious that this is something you're incredibly passionate about. I always enjoy that moment in a conversation when we can truly get to the heart of another person. Such moments often seem odd for the one caught up in them, but I assure you they're delightful to sit and watch. This feels like one of those moments.

Clive: I agree! It seems we've hit a nerve with you Jurgen, and I'm glad we have. Your passion alone persuades me. I think you may be right.

Jean: Me too. You've made it pretty clear. It seems like the alternative is far worse then what you're proposing. I've always just accepted impassibility along with the rest of the "classics," but I think you might be onto something here.

Jurgen: Oh, thank you. I do get carried away sometimes, but you're probably right, it's good to have something to get carried away about.

Well then, how about we take a little break? I've got to run to the toilet.

Clive: Sure, I could go for another tea right about now.

Jean: Alright Jurgen, I think I'm in the right frame of mind to hear what you've got to say about sovereignty. So, let's have it.

Jurgen: Okay, but you don't have to worry too much, friend! I do believe in a sovereign God. I won't be attempting to remove that from the textbooks anytime soon. However, I would like to re-frame the way we tend to understand sovereignty.

I suppose the simplest difference in my understanding of sovereignty is what I've already brought up during the critiques. I avoid determinism like it's the plague, and I suggest the same to you! The main reason is simply that determinism does not look like Jesus, it looks like a Newtonian, deist sort of God. A clockmaker, string puller, and puppet master God. Which in my mind...

Clive: I'd hate to cut in here, but really quick, could you explain what you mean by a Newtonian God? Is that in reference to Sir Isaac Newton? What's wrong with him? I understand the deist stab. Deism believed in an uninvolved, distant God who merely set things into motion for us down here. God then becomes like a morality cop instead of an incarnational Being deeply involved in human affairs. But what's this about Newton?

Jurgen: Well, in my mind, deism and Newton are closely related. Deism actually grew in popularity soon after Newton came forward with his basic cosmology. I think this is due to the general world-view that Newton presented. He gave the world many important ideas about science, but he also got a lot wrong. Albert Einstein corrected much of his cosmology, which I believe was also a great thing for theology.

But generally speaking, Newton theorized that the universe is sort of like a closed system, similar to a clock. Einstein broke that mold with his theory of general relativity. Einstein's theory broke the world free of Newton's closed cosmology which understood the universe as a mechanism. Now, thanks to Einstein, our understanding of the universe is far more robust. The cosmos are not a closed system of harsh rules; the universe is more relative. Time, for instance, is no longer understood as a set standard of measurement; time is relative. In this sense, Newton gave us a closed understanding of the universe, while Einstein gave us an open, more fluid understanding.

The science of history is often reflected in the theology of history. Post-Newton the theological landscape was filled with determinism. World history was understood as a predetermined occurrence. This is why prayer, for example, became a difficult subject. Why would one pray if God has already predetermined all time? Prayer can't change anything if God has already predetermined all time. If time is merely a mechanism in God's clockwork, prayer cannot escape it. This sort of discussion came about through the general determinist framework. Augustine too, I believe, had a hand in the long run in all this. His doctrine of predestination bordered into pre-determinism, or, at least for those persuaded of it, this seemed to be the case.

Since Einstein, science has evolved a great deal towards a more open cosmology. The world is no longer seen in terms of closed systems. Relativity and fluidity are understood now as the core elements of the universe. Theologically speaking, this is a great thing because this speaks back to the non-dualist heritage of Hebraic thought. The Greeks often thought in terms of a dualistic universe, but the Israelites never did.

So this is essentially what I mean when I speak of a Newtonian/deist framework. I am talking about the ways of thinking which have come about through inherent determinism. Newton provided proof for determinism and in turn deism provided a religion for it. Einstein broke the mold, and the Hebraic mind provided a whole new religious context for the universe to be worked out in, theologically speaking. In the current post-Einsteinian era we are in today, theology has followed a more relative understanding of God. I believe this has lead to gaining interest in the doctrine of the Trinity.

Does all that make sense? My science might not be spot on, nor can I tell you how all this has happened, but I think that'll give you the general idea. Thomas F. Torrance once gave an interesting lecture on what he called "The Grounds and Grammar of Theology" that covers this very thing. That's where I've come to familiarize myself with these terms.

Clive: Yes, that's very enlightening. I've never thought about that connection before, but it makes sense that your view of the universe will reflect itself in your theology.

Jean: It is interesting, Jurgen, but I'm still wondering about sovereignty? Drive it home for us: what adjustments are you suggesting?

Jurgen: Alright, I'll say it as simply as I can. To be sovereign is not to be "in control," but to be "in charge." I used to tell my students that God is sovereign like a King, not in control like a dictator. He does not determine the outcome of every single event, but He remains in charge of the earth. He does not cause everything to happen, in all places and at all times, but He is present and Lord over both time and space. Therefore, God is in all things, but He does not determine all things. God is Lord and sovereign over the earth, but this does not equate to total domination of all human history. God does not control the stock market; He gives us freedom in our lives. He remains on the throne, as our king and ultimate concern.

I believe that in the light of Jesus Christ I can say nothing else. When I examine the life of Jesus I do not see the life of one who controls all things. Instead, in Him, I see a God who interacts with the world, not a God who pulls all the strings. The famous prayer Jesus taught His disciples is a great example of this. Jesus says to pray, "Your will be done on earth as it is in heaven," but if God has predetermined all human history, how can God's will not be done already? Why would we pray an arbitrary prayer? Jesus has already spoken in the Sermon on the Mount against needless repetitions in prayer (Matt. 6:7); and so I think this goes to show that the Lord's Prayer is a prayer to a King in charge, not to a dictator who has already predetermined all things.

So that's my understanding of sovereignty. It's a slight change, but I think it has drastic ramifications theologically. For example, when you look at a cancer patient, if you're persuaded of a determinist understanding of the universe, you can do nothing besides tell them that God gave them cancer. Which that conclusion contradicts Jesus Christ who, rather than causing sickness, healed sickness. This is why I said we have to avoid determinism in our understanding of sovereignty. It's dangerous and theologically problematic. It turns God into a monster who causes suffering, instead of the suffering God who meets us in our suffering.

Jean: Okay, but I'm still not sure I'm convinced. How can you say that God is not in control? Isn't it in His nature to be in control of everything? Or are you trying to say that somehow humanity is greater than God, and can go against His will? As Paul asked, "who can resist God's will?" (Romans 9:19). You seem to be saying that everyone can.

Jurgen: God created man in His image correct? So would you say that God is free, inherently?

Jean: Yes, but He's also sovereign, and more importantly, we are not Him.

Jurgen: Yes, I understand that, but wouldn't it be logical to say that since God is free, and we are created in His image, we too are free people with the ability to choose? I think you've taken that passage out of context. I mean, if you sit and examine the stories of the Bible, it seems to me that there are countless examples of people doing exactly what you say they cannot do: resisting God's will.

You may say that ultimately, in the end, even in the worst possible situation, God still uses all things to get His will; but to me, that sounds more like a God who is a King than a God who is a dictator. God may work out all things for the good of those who love Him, but that doesn't mean He makes all things happen. He works all things, that is the key word here! It implies freedom on the part of man to act independently of God.

Jean: I guess I see what you're saying. God's will is the result, but not necessarily the means of getting there. God gets what He wants in the end, but He does not make it happen by force.

Jurgen: Precisely. God did not cause the Holocaust, but God will eventually bring justice there. God will eventually make all things right. There is an eschatological element to all of these terms. God is eternally sovereign. The temporal events of our time are just that: temporary. In the end, God's will be done.

Clive: I like how you put that. I appreciate the injection of freedom into our conversation. I believe that humanity is free and that our freedom is a gift from God. We may not always use freedom appropriately, but in the end, God knows how to work out all things.

Now I hate to say it, but I've got to teach a class soon. This past hour has been a joy, but I need to leave in about fifteen minutes. Would you mind it if we moved on to the last one? What did you say it was again, Jurgen?

Jurgen: Immutability: the doctrine that God cannot change. It's a good thing we saved this one for last; I have the least to say about it.

Generally speaking, I affirm this to be true. But I'm afraid that in its common context, the immutability of God has been misused and misinterpreted. Originally, this doctrine was developed against the Arian heresy. The creed of Nicaea responded with the statement: God is not changeable. But I don't believe this statement was ever meant to be absolute. It is only used here as a simile. God is not changeable in the same way that creatures are changeable, but this also does not imply that God is unchangeable in every single respect. The statement that God is unchangeable deals with the notion that God is unchangeable by that which is not God. We cannot change God, nor can any created force or event enact a change in God. However, the statement that God is unchangeable does not imply that God is intrinsically unchangeable. Rather, it means that God cannot be changed by an outside force acting upon Him. Therefore, this statement originally implies that God cannot be changed by an outside force. However, it was never intended to mean that God cannot change Himself, nor that God is not free to make Himself open to being acted upon by an outside force. So while it is true that God cannot be changed, this does not mean that God is absolutely unchangeable because in His freedom

God is perfectly capable of changing Himself and making Himself open to the change of others.

Now of course, this does not imply that God is schizophrenic. God can change Himself but He cannot go back on His Word to the human race. Jesus Christ remains the absolute revelation of God forever. We are not at the risk of meeting a God behind the back of Jesus Christ who is different from Jesus Christ. God is like Jesus and Jesus is like God. This is the promise of the covenant. God is the God of promise, and this makes Him adamantly bound to the human race. And so, this discussion does not imply that God can at any minute change His mind about the human race and turn His back in disgrace. We belong to God and this will never change because Jesus Christ has promised it.

However, it's important to clarify the immutability of God because when taken too far this concept can sometimes lead to problematic thinking. A God who cannot change in the absolute sense of the term is a God with deterministic tendencies. This is the problem with taking this statement outside of its original bounds. Yes, God is unchangeable, but God can change Himself. This implies that the Godhead is fluid rather than mechanistic. The God of deism is a God who stands far away from humanity like a puppet master pulling our strings. The immutability of God runs the risk of this perception whenever it forgets the fact that while God is unchangeable, God remains free to change Himself. God is not a mechanism; God is a fluid dance. God is a love affair between the Father, Son, and Holy Spirit. Perichoresis, the inner relationship of God, is central to our doctrine of the Trinity. Unfortunately, I have found that the idea of an unchanging God (an "unmoved mover") has taken the place of God as a Trinitarian dance. God is perceived therefore less as a fellowship of love and more as a master computer. But I believe there is hope in the current theological trend, which I see moving more towards a Trinitarian emphasis.

In a summary then, a God who cannot change is a robotic God, while a God who is free to change Himself is a Trinitarian relationship. In the light of Jesus Christ, we have to recapture the Trinitarian nature of God as a relational Being, rather than as a mechanistic deity.

So while it may seem like a technicality to you all, it matters to me. An unchanging God can take away from the Trinity. Far be it for me to take away God's freedom to be God, and His freedom to define what that means. For this reason, I redefine immutability in this way.

But anyways, gentleman, this has been a treat. I've greatly enjoyed getting to explain myself to you. I hope it wasn't too much to handle. Let me know if there are any questions that come up during the week. Next, I'd like to talk briefly about some of the eschatological implications to all this, would that be alright? After that, we can move on to something else, but if we're going to do justice to this topic I believe we need to examine one more thing. We can meet at the same time. I'm afraid Friedrich probably won't be able to make it again. But we'll wrap it up before he returns, and pick a new subject for him to jump in on.

Jean: Thank you Jurgen, this has been interesting. Next week sounds great as well. I'll see you then.

Clive: Good-bye! I've got to run. But I agree, next week sounds great.

THE LAST CHATPER

Clive: I'm afraid to say it Jurgen, but I think last week got us away from the original purpose of this discussion. Didn't it seem a little too... I don't know, theoretical? Weren't we trying to be practical, to speak with the Holocaust in mind?

Jurgen: Yes, you're very right. Unfortunately, we did get off a bit, but I honestly don't regret that we did. I'm glad we had the discussion we had last time. But, although abstract discussions have their place, true theology must be practical theology, you are correct. Abstract thinking helps almost no one. So let's try to be more practical today, alright?

I'd rather like to hear what you two have to say. I've talked enough already. So answer me this: Where was God in the Holocaust?—this was our original dilemma, and I propose we start here one last time. Jean, any thoughts?

Jean: Where was God? God was in the Holocaust, and the Holocaust was in God. God did not cause the event to happen, nor did He will for its happening. God met humanity in this event, and in fact, He has met us in all things. God, in His power, becomes weak; in His sovereignty, becomes a servant. God undoes suffering from within. God suffers with victims of suffering, and therefore, God overcomes suffering itself. God overcomes the evil of the Holocaust by joining Himself to our humanity in the suffering and death that has happened there.

Clive: Well said, Jean. I'd like you all to know, I took your suggestion and read E. Wiesel's book *Night*. It was truly profound, especially as I pondered this discussion. Would you mind if I read a quote?

Jurgen: Of course not, go right ahead.

Clive: Thank you. This scene depicts the hanging of a small boy from the prison camp. It's horrific to think about, but there's one line that stood out to me as I read it:

> Then came the march past the victims. The two men were no longer alive. Their tongues were hanging out, swollen and bluish. But the third rope was still moving: the child, too light, was still breathing [...] And so he remained for more than half an hour, lingering between life and death, writhing before our eyes. And we were forced to look at him at close range. He was still alive when I passed him. His tongue was still red, his eyes not yet extinguished. Behind me, I heard the same man asking: 'For God's sake, where is God?' And from within me, I heard a voice answer: 'Where He is? This is where —hanging here from this gallows...'"

> — NIGHT, 64

Jean: Dear God... That's moving; deeply moving. I must have missed that back in university when I read it.

Jurgen: That's my favorite line in the entire book! Well, as much as it is impossible to have a "favorite" line in a book about such a tragedy. But this line influenced me a great deal as I developed this theodicy. It's not a pleasant line, but it is important.

Clive: I think it goes right in the same line of thought as your thesis, Jurgen. I now see that if we take the person of Jesus Christ seriously enough, as the crucified Christ, then we cannot answer our dilemma in any other way. Where is God? God is there, in the pages of human history, with us in our existence, making our existence a part of Himself. God is suffering with every victim, with the oppressed, the destitute, the broken, the weak, and the dying. Even in death, God finds us. Perhaps this is what the Psalmist was getting at when he sang, "If I ascend to heaven, you are there! If I make my bed in Sheol, behold, you are there!" (Ps. 139:8). God has truly reached the human race in all our darkness and sin!

Jurgen: God suffers with humanity, this is the startling fact that we must deduce from the crucifixion of Jesus Christ. We cannot say (as the Greek philosophers do) that suffering and pain are foreign to God. He has taken our sufferings upon Himself, and suffers in our sufferings. God has taken our joys upon Himself, and He takes delight in our joy. One author writes that, "If that is to be taken seriously [that history is in God], it must also mean that, like the cross, even Auschwitz is in God himself. Even Auschwitz is taken up into the grief of the Father, the surrender of the Son and the power of the Spirit" (*The Crucified God*, 278).

Jean: Well, I think that just about answers our question then. And what a wonderful answer indeed! It's truly encouraging to hear it. God does not cause the Holocaust, and He is not removed from the Holocaust either. God is in the Holocaust. God suffered and died there. And this suffering and death is the paradoxical power of God. God overcomes by assumption, heals by participation, and raises the dead by being dead Himself!

Jurgen: Very well said, but I have to add one more thing to our discussion. If we're truly going to be thorough, we must also consider the eschatological implications at hand here. Eschatology, the study of the last things, is not a footnote to theology. Instead, the reality of the coming of God must be taken seriously in all theology. "From first to last, and not merely in the epilogue, Christianity is eschatology, is hope, forward looking and forward moving" (*Theology of Hope*, 16).

Clive: Eschatology? Like the anti-Christ and rapture stuff? I wouldn't have pegged you as an eschatologist, Jurgen!

Jurgen: Well I'm not, I'm a theologian. But I believe that all theology should be eschatological. I am not talking about "pop" eschatology, rapture theories and time-lines are for the unlearned. No theologian I know would take any of those things seriously.

Instead, what I mean here are the final things which are to come.

Namely, the coming Kingdom of God and the fulfillment of God's reign. We live in this tension, knowing that while we have the Gospel and the fullness of the Godhead available to us, we also have a hope for the full manifestation of the Kingdom. The Kingdom is at hand, Jesus said, and the Kingdom is coming. Both are true, and this is the "now but not yet" reality we live in. Therefore, theologically speaking, we should work out our ideas in an eschatologically way which brings hope for the coming of God and His Kingdom. We live expectant and in the pull of these promises. We live with hope. One author writes that "to live without hope is to cease to live. Hell is hopelessness. It is no accident that above the entrance to Dante's hell is the inscription 'Leave behind all hope, you who enter here'" (*Theology of Hope*, 90). We must be theologians of hope. And to be this, we must preach eschatology.

Jean: But how can the Holocaust be an eschatological event?

Jurgen: Because there is hope, even in the darkest places. Even in Hitler's gas chambers, there is hope for his victims, a hope found in the light of the crucifixion. If God meets us in our suffering on Good Friday, then on Resurrection Sunday our suffering is overcome. This brings hope to all humanity. Suffering will not have the final word, nor will death. God has overcome the world, truly. God in Christ has suffered as we suffer and died as we all will one day die. But He has also risen to life, to a New Creation! This is our hope. God does not only suffers in our sufferings; He overcomes our sufferings with resurrection life. This is the eschatological event the whole world is waiting for. We see historically in this man Jesus Christ the resurrection of God, but in this event, we also see the promise of the resurrection of all things. The resurrection is the hope of a new life, of a "beyond" for us to go to.

The resurrection of Jesus Christ is the good news that suffering and evil will not win—that even in our darkest moment there is light. Even the Holocaust is not without hope. All things have become new in Christ Jesus, and they're becoming new in the eschatological resurrection which is to come.

Simply, the resurrection of Jesus Christ speaks to all people in all times that "God is my beyond." That is, in the midst of suffering and death, God is our collective beyond. He holds our life secure in death. What else could you think of that is the ultimate equalizer? Every human being dies, and therefore God meets all humanity in death. And from our death, God creates a new world. This is the New Creation to come, the resurrection of all things, which is fulfilled in the coming of God and His Kingdom. This is the eschatological hope we're talking about here.

Clive: If I understand you correctly, you seem to be saying that the resurrection of Jesus Christ is the promise of a future which belongs to God? That His resurrection is the future of humanity; that in the same pattern of His raising we too we all one day be raised to life from the dead?

Jurgen: Exactly! And it's not just about humanity; all things will become new including history, including the Holocaust. All things will be made new! In the "last chapter" of humanity, the wrongs of the world will be made right. The dead will be raised to life, and at last the dark days of humanity will be a forgotten memory. This is what the justice of God is all about. Justice sets things right. In the end, God will do just that.

Jean: I like that, Jurgen. I think there is something to be said about taking eschatology seriously, especially when dealing with theodicy. The problem of human suffering and God often is set up in terms which are anything but eschatological. I think if the church took eschatology more seriously, as the hope of God's coming Kingdom, then we wouldn't have such a hard time with the present sufferings of our world. We, of course, wouldn't justify—or worse yet, glorify suffering and death, but, instead, we would see suffering and death as events in the life of God.

Clive: Yes, I believe that would help move us forward. We can often get too stuck in arguments and apologetics that we forget to see the conclusion of it all. Even in the act of trying to "prove" God to another human being, there is an eschatological element. Ultimately, God will prove Himself. We often act as if it is our Christian duty to prove the existence of God to an unbelieving world! We take little seriousness to the fact that God is God and He is more than capable of proving Himself. And He will! That eschatological element would certainly get us past many of the present day arguments and divisions that take place between Christians and the world. Rather than continually attempting to argue men and women into the fellowship of the saints, we should love them in, knowing full well that God will prove Himself in the end. In that faithful last chapter of humanity, God will show the world that He is good, that He is just, and that He is madly in love with us all.

Jurgen: That's a good way of looking at it. Too often I'm afraid the Christian church acts as if its mission is to convince the world of something rather than proclaim to the world someone. I am persuaded that if we could move past arguments and proofs, we might be able to, once again, preach only Christ and Him crucified. The proclamation of the Gospel is essential to the church. We seem to have lost sight of that. And you're right, a proper emphasis on eschatology may move the church forward into a new season where we focus less on proving God and more on proclaiming the Gospel.

Clive: This is all great stuff, but unfortunately we're just about out of time. We'll have to be quick as we close. So how about a brief summary of these last four weeks? And before I forget to mention it, Friedrich said he will be back with us next week and promises to come with a new topic for discussion.

Jean: Oh good, I've missed him. I'm excited to hear what he says. But for now, how about Jurgen you give us a summary?

Jurgen: Alright, I'll read one from John's Gospel: "So they took Jesus, and he went out, bearing his own cross, to the place called The Place of a Skull, which in Aramaic is called Golgatha. There they crucified him, and with him two others, one on either side, and Jesus between them. […] When Jesus had received the sour wine, he said, 'It is finished,' and he bowed his head and gave up his spirit" (John 19:16b-18, 30 ESV). Amen!

Clive & Jean: Amen!

EPILOGUE

In this short book, I have attempted to make a specific case for the Holocaust and God's relation to it. I initially thought I would present my arguments in the usual manner that nonfiction books often present them in, but I found myself bored by my own process. So to make this book more interesting, both for myself and for you, the reader, I decided to make this a written dialogue amongst four fictional friends. Each voice in this book represents a general response to the Holocaust dilemma. They also represent a historical person who's famous for that specific response. My view is expressed in Jurgen, who's named after the theologian Jürgen Moltmann. Moltmann is the author of *The Crucified God* and *Theology of Hope*. Both books have tremendously impacted the thought of this book, as well as my life personally. Therefore, Jurgen seemed like the best character to portray my thoughts.

The other characters may or may not have been more apparent. Clive stood in for C.S. Lewis (Clive being his first name). I found C.S. Lewis' approach to theodicy in *The Problem of Pain* to be more of an apologetic defense for God, and less like an actual theodicy. As was brought up in this book, C.S. Lewis never really answered the question of suffering, but instead, he gave what is more like a defense for God.

That's why Clive took the position he did, which ultimately had to appeal to mystery.

Jean stood for John Calvin since Jean is the French version of John. John Calvin, the reformer, is someone I greatly admire. But I am afraid to say his theology borders determinism far too much (especially within the realms of sovereignty and election). This is why Jean represents the determinist position, which is sometimes found in Calvinism (but not always).

Friedrich stood for Friedrich Nietzsche, famous for pioneering the "God is dead" movement. He obviously took the position of atheism. Although I've never read anything from Nietzsche myself, I am familiar enough with his general work to know that he fits nicely in this book to represent an atheist's response to the Holocaust.

Each character is a *symbol* and not a literal representation. I promise you that if any four of these men were to read this book, they would probably be appalled at the words I have put in their mouths! For this reason, the characters are not literally meant to be these specific individuals. Instead, I use their general way of thinking (as I understand them) to present my arguments in this book.

Jurgen presents my overall position and the way I would personally argue against an atheist or determinist position. Jurgen's discussions with Clive are my engagements with C.S. Lewis and those who discuss theodicy in similar ways. C.S. Lewis is the closest of the three positions to my own, but Jurgen Moltmann is the truest theodicy of the bunch. In later chapters both Jean and Clive present my voice, but I hope that has already become apparent.

In *The Crucified God*, Jurgen Moltmann offers the theological basis for my position: that God is in our person holocausts and our holocausts are in God. The discussions about impassibility, immutability, and omnipotence are also from the works of Moltmann.

Of course, everything is put into my own words, so this certainly is not to say that I have merely re-stated Moltmann's work. Instead, I attempted to emphasize The Crucified God as an important response to the Holocaust event. This work served as a foundation which I built upon.

I chose the Holocaust for the practical backdrop in this book because I was deeply moved by E. Wiesel's book *Night*. A combination of Moltmann's theology and the moving account found in *Night* lead to this book being written. I wanted to write this simple book to give hope to all those who suffer and are affected by pain. My prayer is that this book can be a source of comfort and hope. I also hope that it will answer some of the tough questions. While I don't believe that every question can be answered (especially in a book as short as this one!), I do hope that here I can at least offer my contribution to the theodicy discussion.

Ultimately, this is my goal for this book: that some might find hope in suffering.

The God of the crucified Christ is our Lord and Father, and He has met us in our sufferings. He has overcome. We are over-comers in Him.

This is the hope of the Gospel for a world drowning in suffering and death. God is with us, history is in God, and there is hope in the resurrection of a new world beyond this one. Pain and suffering will not have the final word, the crucified and risen Christ does. The final word of the Almighty God in the midst of our death and suffering is a triumphant "it is finished!"

S. D. Morrison

FURTHER READING

Jesus Christ for Today's World by Jürgen Moltmann for a general introduction to his most important contributions to theology.

The Crucified God by Jürgen Moltmann for a groundbreaking theological engagement in the cross of Jesus Christ as the hope for humanity.

The Trinity and the Kingdom by Jürgen Moltmann for an excellent study of the doctrine of God.

Theology of Hope by Jurgen Moltmann for the importance of Eschatology.

Against Heresies Book III by Irenaeus of Lyons for a nuanced discussion of impassibility and the suffering of Jesus Christ. See specifically chapters 11 section 7 and 16 section 6.

The Epistle to the Romans by Karl Barth for his famous critique of natural theology.

ABOUT THE AUTHOR

STEPHEN D. MORRISON is a prolific American writer, ecumenical theologian, novelist, artist, and literary critic. A strong sense of creativity and curiosity drives his productive output of books on a wide range of subjects.

This book is the third in his "Plain English Series." Previous volumes include *Karl Barth in Plain English* and *T. F. Torrance in Plain English*.

For more on Stephen, please visit his website. There you can stay up to date with his latest projects and ongoing thoughts.

———

WWW.SDMORRISON.ORG

ALSO BY STEPHEN D. MORRISON

www.ingramcontent.com/pod-product-compliance
Lightning Source LLC
Chambersburg PA
CBHW061509040426
42450CB00008B/1539